The Nursery Rhymes of Winnie the Pooh

A Classic Disney Treasury

SCHOLASTIC INC.

New York Toronto London Auckland Sydney
Mexico City New Delhi Hong Kong

ISBN 0-439-12955-9

Copyright © 1998 by Disney Enterprises, Inc.
All rights reserved.
Published by Scholastic Inc., 555 Broadway, New York, NY 10012,
by arrangement with Disney Press, an imprint of Buena Vista Books, Inc.
SCHOLASTIC and associated logos are trademarks and/or registered
trademarks of Scholastic Inc.

12 11 10 9 8 7 6 5 4 3 2 1   9/9 0 1 2 3 4/0

Printed in the Mexico   49

First Scholastic printing, September 1999

Based on the Pooh stories by A.A. Milne (copyright The Pooh Properties Trust.)

The Nursery Rhymes of
Winnie the Pooh

Table of Contents

4

A-hunting we will go,
a-hunting we will go.
Hi, ho, the merry-o,
a-hunting we will go.

Are You Sleeping?

Are you sleeping, are you sleeping,
Brother John, Brother John?
Morning bells are ringing,
Morning bells are ringing.
Ding, ding, dong.
Ding, ding, dong.

Baa Baa Black Sheep

Baa baa black sheep, have you any wool?

Yes, sir, yes, sir, three bags full.

One for my master, one for the dame,

And one for the little boy who lives down the lane.

Bye Baby Bunting

Bye baby bunting,

Father's gone a-hunting

To catch a little rabbit skin

To put bye baby bunting in.

Clap, Clap, Clap Your Hands

Clap, clap, clap your hands,

Clap your hands together.

Clap, clap, clap your hands,

Clap your hands right now.

Did You Ever See a Laddie?

Did you ever see a laddie,

a laddie, a laddie?

Did you ever see a laddie

go this way and that?

Go this way and that way,

go this way and that way.

Did you ever see a laddie

go this way and that?

The Farmer in the Dell

The farmer in the dell, the farmer in the dell,

Hi, ho, the derry-o, the farmer in the dell.

The farmer takes a wife, the farmer takes a wife,

Hi, ho, the derry-o, the farmer takes a wife.

The wife takes a child, the wife takes a child,

Hi, ho, the derry-o, the wife takes a child.

The child takes a nurse, the child takes a nurse,

Hi, ho, the derry-o, the child takes a nurse.

The nurse takes a dog, the nurse takes a dog,

Hi, ho, the derry-o, the nurse takes a dog.

The dog takes a cat, the dog takes a cat,

Hi, ho, the derry-o, the dog takes a cat.

The cat takes a mouse, the cat takes a mouse,

Hi, ho, the derry-o, the cat takes a mouse.

The mouse takes the cheese, the mouse takes the cheese,

Hi, ho, the derry-o, the mouse takes the cheese.

The cheese stands alone, the cheese stands alone,

Hi, ho, the derry-o, the cheese stands alone.

Head and Shoulders, Knees and Toes

Head and shoulders, knees and toes, knees and toes.

Head and shoulders, knees and toes, knees and toes.

Eyes and ears and mouth and nose.

Head and shoulders, knees and toes, knees and toes.

Here We Go 'Round the Mulberry Bush

Here we go 'round the mulberry bush,
the mulberry bush, the mulberry bush.
Here we go 'round the mulberry bush,
so early in the morning.

Hey Diddle Diddle

Hey diddle diddle,
the cat and the fiddle.

The cow jumped over the moon.

The little dog laughed to see such a sight,

And the dish ran away with the spoon.

Hickory, Dickory, Dock

Hickory, dickory, dock!
The mouse ran up the clock.
The clock struck one,
The mouse ran down,
Hickory, dickory, dock!

Hush, Little Baby

Hush, little baby, don't say a word,

Momma's gonna buy you a mockingbird.

If that mockingbird won't sing,

Momma's gonna buy you a diamond ring.

If that diamond ring turns brass,

Momma's gonna buy you a looking glass.

If that looking glass gets broke,

Momma's gonna buy you a billy goat.

If that billy goat won't pull,

Momma's gonna buy you a cart and bull.

If that cart and bull turn over,

Momma's gonna buy you a dog named Rover.

If that dog named Rover won't bark,

Momma's gonna buy you a horse and cart.

If that horse and cart fall down,

you'll still be the sweetest little baby in town.

I Am Walking

I am walking, walking, walking,

I am walking, walking, walking,

I am walking, walking, walking,

I am walking, walking, walking,

Now I stop.

I'm a Little Teapot

I'm a little teapot, short and stout.

Here is my handle, here is my spout.

When I get all steamed up, hear me shout,

"Just tip me over and pour me out."

If You're Happy and You Know It

If you're happy and you know it,
clap your hands.

Clap, clap.

If you're happy and you know it,
clap your hands.

Clap, clap.

If you're happy and you know it,
Then your face will surely show it.

If you're happy and you know it,
clap your hands.

Clap, clap.

If you're happy and you know it,
stamp your feet.

Stamp, stamp.

If you're happy and you know it,
stamp your feet.

Stamp, stamp.

If you're happy and you know it,

Then your face will surely show it.

If you're happy and you know it,

stamp your feet.

Stamp, stamp.

If you're happy and you know it,
nod your head.

Nod, nod.

If you're happy and you know it,
nod your head.

Nod, nod

If you're happy and you know it,
Then your face will surely show it.
If you're happy and you know it,
nod your head.

Nod, nod.

If you're happy and you know it,
pat your knees.

Pat , pat.

If you're happy and you know it,
pat your knees.

Pat , pat.

If you're happy and you know it,
Then your face will surely show it.
If you're happy and you know it,
pat your knees.

Pat , pat.

In a Cabin, in the Woods

In a cabin, in the woods,

Little old man by the window stood.

Saw a rabbit hopping by,

Knocking at his door.

"Help me, help me!" the rabbit said,

"Or the hunter will catch me instead!"

Little rabbit, come inside;

Safely you'll abide.

It's Raining, It's Pouring

It's raining, it's pouring,

The old man is snoring.

He went to bed

And bumped his head,

And didn't wake up till morning.

The Itsy-Bitsy Spider

The itsy-bitsy spider went up the water spout.

Down came the rain
and washed the spider out.

Out came the sun
and dried up all the rain.
And the itsy-bitsy spider
went up the spout again.

Jack and Jill

Jack and Jill went up the hill
To fetch a pail of water.
Jack fell down and broke his crown,
And Jill came tumbling after.

Jack Be Nimble

Jack be nimble,

Jack be quick,

Jack jump over the candlestick.

Ladybug, Ladybug, Fly Away Home

Ladybug, ladybug, fly away home.

Your house is on fire, your children are gone.

All except one, her name is Nan.

She crept under a frying pan.

Lazy Mary

Lazy Mary, will you get up,

Will you get up,

Will you get up?

Lazy Mary, will you get up,

Will you get up this

morning?

Little Duckie Duddle

Little Duckie Duddle

Went wading in a puddle,

Went wading in a puddle quite small.

Said he, "It doesn't matter

How much I splash and splatter,

I'm only a duckie, after all. Quack, quack."

Little Green Frog

Ah—ump, went the little green frog one day.

Ah—ump, went the little green frog.

Ah—ump, went the little green frog one day.

And his green eyes went *blink, blink, blink.*

Little Jack Horner

Little Jack Horner sat in a corner,

Eating his Christmas pie.

He stuck in his thumb and pulled out a plum,

And said, "What a good boy am I."

London Bridge

London Bridge is falling down, falling down,
   falling down,
London Bridge is falling down, my fair lady.
Take the key and lock him up, lock him up,
   lock him up,
Take the key and lock him up, my fair lady.

Mary Had a Little Lamb

Mary had a little lamb,

Little lamb, little lamb,

Mary had a little lamb

Whose fleece was white as snow.

Everywhere that Mary went,

Mary went, Mary went,

Everywhere that Mary went

The lamb was sure to go.

It followed her to school one day,

School one day, school one day.

It followed her to school one day,

Which was against the rules.

It made the children laugh and play,

Laugh and play, laugh and play.

It made the children laugh and play

To see a lamb at school.

Mary, Mary, Quite Contrary

Mary, Mary, quite contrary,
How does your garden grow?

"With silver bells and cockle shells
And pretty maids all in a row."

54

Miss Mary Mack

Miss Mary Mack, Mack, Mack,

All dressed in black, black, black,

With silver buttons, buttons, buttons,

All down her back, back, back.

She asked her mother, mother, mother,

For fifteen cents, cents, cents,

To see the elephant, elephant, elephant,

Jump over the fence, fence, fence.

He jumped so high, high, high,

He touched the sky, sky, sky,

And didn't come back, back, back,

Until the Fourth of July, -ly, -ly.

Miss Polly Had a Dolly

Miss Polly had a dolly that was
     sick, sick, sick,
So she telephoned the doctor to come
     quick, quick, quick.
The doctor came with her bag and her cap.
And she knocked on the door with a
     rat-a-tat-tat.
She looked at the dolly and she shook her head.
"Miss Polly, put that dolly straight to
     bed, bed, bed."
She wrote on the paper for the
     pill, pill, pill,
"I'll be back tomorrow with the
     bill, bill, bill!"

Muffin Man

Do you know the muffin man,
   the muffin man,
   the muffin man?
Do you know the muffin man
   who lives on Drury Lane?
Yes I know the muffin man,
   the muffin man,
   the muffin man.
Yes I know the muffin man,
   who lives on Drury lane.

Oats, Peas, Beans

Oats, peas, beans, and barley grow;

Oats, peas, beans, and barley grow;

Do you or I or anyone know

How oats, peas, beans, and barley grow?

Old King Cole

Old King Cole was a merry old soul,

And a merry old soul was he.

He called for his pipe and he called for his bowl,

And he called for his fiddlers three.

Old MacDonald

Old MacDonald had a farm,
    E-I-E-I-O.
And on his farm he had a pig,
    E-I-E-I-O.
With an oink oink here
And an oink oink there
Here an oink, there an oink,
Everywhere an oink oink,
Old MacDonald had a farm,
    E-I-E-I-O.

62

Open, Shut Them

Open, shut them, open, shut them,
  give a little clap.
Open, shut them, open, shut them,
  lay them in your lap.
Creep them, creep them, creep them,
  creep them right up to your chin.
Open wide your little mouth, but do not let
  them in.

Pat-a-Cake

Pat-a-cake, pat-a-cake, baker's man,

Bake me a cake as fast as you can.

Pat it and roll it and mark it with a B,

And put it in the oven for baby and me.

Pease Porridge Hot

Pease porridge hot, pease porridge cold,

Pease porridge in the pot, nine days old.

Some like it hot, some like it cold,

Some like it in the pot, nine days old.

Pop Goes the Weasel

Round and 'round the mulberry bush

The monkey chased the weasel.

The monkey thought 'twas all in fun.

Pop goes the weasel.

Ring Around the Rosy

Ring around the rosy,
A pocket full of posies.
Ashes, ashes,
We all fall down.

Rock-a-Bye Baby

Rock-a-bye baby, in the tree top,

When the wind blows, the cradle will rock.

When the bough breaks, the cradle will fall,

And down will come baby, cradle, and all.

Row, Row, Row Your Boat

Row, row, row your boat
Gently down the stream.
Merrily, merrily, merrily, merrily,
Life is but a dream.

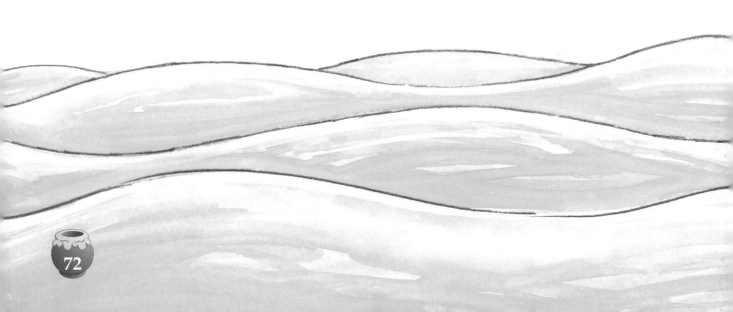

Rub-a-dub-dub

Rub-a-dub-dub, three men in a tub,
And who do you think they be?
The butcher, the baker,
　　the candlestick maker.
Turn them out, knaves all three.

See saw, Margery Daw,

   Johnny shall have a new master.

He shall have but a penny a day

   because he can't work any faster.

Shoe the Horse

Shoe the horse, shoe the horse,

Shoe the bay mare.

Here a nail, there a nail,

Still she stands there.

Sing a Song of Sixpence

Sing a song of sixpence, a pocket full of rye.

Four and twenty blackbirds baked in a pie.

When the pie was opened

   the birds began to sing.

Wasn't that a dainty dish to set before the king?

Swing Our Hands

Swing our hands, swing our hands,
swing our hands together.

Swing our hands, swing our hands,
in our circle now.
Tap our toes, tap our toes,
tap our toes together.
Tap our toes, tap our toes,
in our circle now.

Teddy Bear

Teddy bear, teddy bear, turn around,

Teddy bear, teddy bear, touch the ground.

Teddy bear, teddy bear, show your shoe,

Teddy bear, teddy bear, that will do!

There Was a Duke of York

There was a duke of York.

He had ten thousand men.

He marched them up the hill.

And then he marched them down again.

When you're up, you're up.

And when you're down, you're down.

And when you're only halfway up

You're neither up nor down.

This Is the Way We Wash Our Clothes

This is the way we wash our clothes,

wash our clothes, wash our clothes.

This is the way we wash our clothes,
so early in the morning.

This Little Piggy

This little piggy went to market,
    and this little piggy stayed home;
This little piggy had roast beef,
    and this little piggy had none;
And this little piggy cried,
    Wee, wee, wee, all the way home.

Twinkle, Twinkle, Little Star

Twinkle, twinkle, little star.

How I wonder what you are.

Up above the world so high,

Like a diamond in the sky.

Twinkle, twinkle, little star

How I wonder what you are.

Wheels on the Bus

The wheels on the bus go round and round,
round and round, round and round.
The wheels on the bus go round and round
all through the town.
The baby on the bus goes, Wah wah wah,
wah wah wah, wah wah wah.
The baby on the bus goes Wah wah wah,
all through the town.
The lights on the bus go blink blink blink,
blink blink blink, blink blink blink,
The light on the bus go blink blink blink,
all through the town.

The driver on the bus says,

"Move on back, move on back, move on back,"

The driver on the bus says,

"Move on back," all through the town.

The money on the bus goes, clink clink clink,
  clink clink clink, clink clink clink,
The money on the bus goes, clink clink clink,
  all through the town.

The people on the bus go up and down,
up and down, up and down,
The people on the bus go up and down,
all through the town.

The wipers on the bus go, swish swish swish,
swish swish swish, swish swish swish,
The wipers on the bus go, swish swish swish,
all through the town.

Where Is Thumbkin?

Where is Thumbkin?

Where is Thumbkin?

Here I am, here I am.

How are you today, sir?

Very well, I thank you.

Run away, run away.

Where, Oh Where Is Pretty Little Susie?

Where, oh where is pretty little Susie?

Where, oh where is pretty little Susie?

Where, oh where is pretty little Susie?

Way down yonder in the pawpaw patch.

Yankee Doodle

Oh, Yankee Doodle went to town,
    a-riding on a pony;
He stuck a feather in his cap
    and called it macaroni.
Yankee Doodle keep it up;
    Yankee Doodle Dandy,
Mind the music and the step,
    and with the girls be handy.